lonely planet
Kids

The Plastic Problem

60 SMALL WAYS TO REDUCE WASTE AND SAVE THE EARTH

AUBRE ANDRUS

CONTENTS

PLASTIC, PLASTIC EVERYWHERE!

It's very likely that you use plastic many, many times every day.

But you probably don't know much about it.

What is it? Where did it come from? And why do we use it?

WHAT IS PLASTIC?

Plastic can be soft or hard, clear or colored, recyclable or not. Have you ever noticed a number stamped on a plastic item? It tells you which kind of plastic it is. Some are better for the environment—and your body—than others.

Name: PETE or PET (Polyethylene Terephthalate)

Easy to Recycle? Yes.

Safe to Reuse? No. PETE absorbs bacteria and flavors, so it is too hard to clean after it's been used. That means you shouldn't use a plastic water bottle more than once.

SODA BOTTLE

CONDIMENT BOTTLE

WATER BOTTLE

2 HDPE

Name: HDPE or PE-HE (High-density Polyethylene)

Easy to Recycle? Yes.

Safe to Reuse? Yes.

LAUNDRY DETERGENT

SHAMPOO BOTTLE

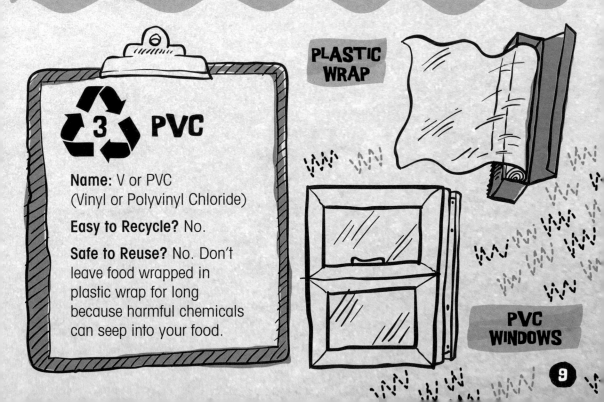

3 PVC

Name: V or PVC (Vinyl or Polyvinyl Chloride)

Easy to Recycle? No.

Safe to Reuse? No. Don't leave food wrapped in plastic wrap for long because harmful chemicals can seep into your food.

PLASTIC WRAP

PVC WINDOWS

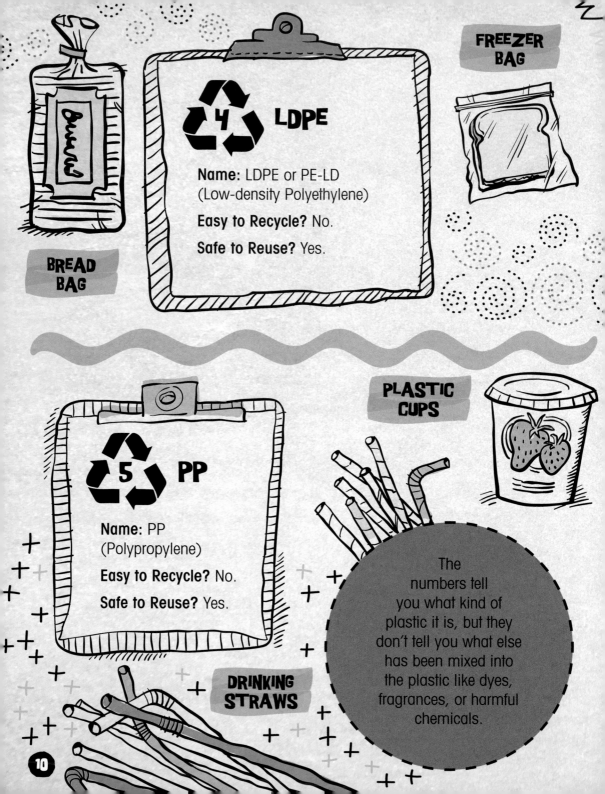

FREEZER BAG

LDPE
♺ 4

Name: LDPE or PE-LD (Low-density Polyethylene)

Easy to Recycle? No.

Safe to Reuse? Yes.

BREAD BAG

PLASTIC CUPS

PP
♺ 5

Name: PP (Polypropylene)

Easy to Recycle? No.

Safe to Reuse? Yes.

DRINKING STRAWS

The numbers tell you what kind of plastic it is, but they don't tell you what else has been mixed into the plastic like dyes, fragrances, or harmful chemicals.

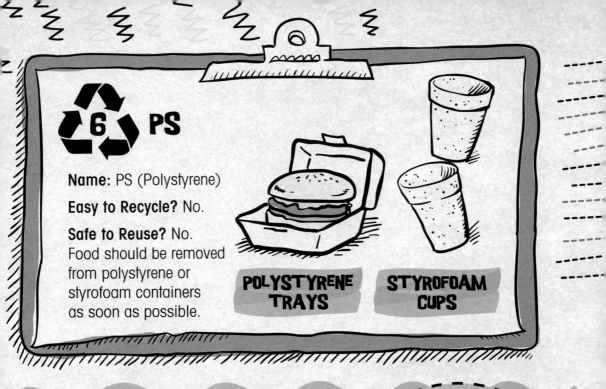

6 PS

Name: PS (Polystyrene)

Easy to Recycle? No.

Safe to Reuse? No.
Food should be removed
from polystyrene or
styrofoam containers
as soon as possible.

POLYSTYRENE TRAYS

STYROFOAM CUPS

7 OTHER

Name: OTHER or O (A catch-all
category for Polycarbonate, BPA,
and more)

Easy to Recycle? No.

Safe to Reuse? No. Don't store
food in containers made from
plastic #7. Unsafe chemicals,
like BPA, can enter into your food.

So,
which plastic
is the best? The best
plastics for you and the
environment are #5, #2,
and #1 (as long as you
don't reuse it)! Number 4
is fine for you, but
not great for the
environment.

PLASTIC SUNGLASSES

11

PLASTIC THROUGHOUT HISTORY

About 150 years ago, plastic was a really great invention that solved a lot of problems. But the benefits of plastic come at a cost—a cost that is too great for our planet and for our own health.

1860s

Wild elephants were being killed for their ivory tusks, which were then used to make billiard balls and piano keys. American inventor Wesley Hyatt wanted to change that. He created a plant-based plastic called celluloid to replace ivory. It was a hit!

1900s-1930s

Belgian Leo Baekeland invented another kind of plastic called Bakelite, which could be molded into any shape and easily mass-produced. It was the first fully synthetic plastic, meaning it was made from materials that aren't found in nature. It was also the first plastic derived from fossil fuels. See page 30 for more about fossil fuels.

1950s

Two toy inventors learned that kids in Australia were twirling wooden hoops around their waists for fun. They decided to make a plastic version and sell it to kids in the States. Wham-O's Hula Hoop became insanely popular.

1980s

Swatch, a mostly plastic watch, was introduced. It was cheaper than other watches and very colorful. Instead of having just one nice watch, people were encouraged to buy a watch to match every outfit!

2010s

3D printing machines used melted plastic to "print" objects slice by slice from the bottom up. The melted layers hardened together to create solid objects like vases, toys, and machine parts.

TODAY

Now plastic is used to make stadium seating, baby bottles, notebook binders, airplanes, outdoor furniture, trash bags, water bottles, and much more. As the years go by, we're realizing that we've created too much of it. What started as a great solution has now turned into a major problem.

WHERE IS PLASTIC?

When you think about plastic, bottles and bags probably come to mind. But plastic is found in many places that you may not expect.

IN YOUR ELECTRONICS

Phones, keyboards, computers, video game systems—they're all made of plastic! So are TVs and their remotes.

IN YOUR CAR

Cars have a lot of plastic on their insides as well as a protective layer of plastic on the glass windshield. Plastics help absorb the impact of a crash much more than metals do.

IN YOUR CLOTHES

A majority of clothing is made from synthetic fabrics like nylon or polyester, which are types of plastic. It may even be covering the couch or chairs in your living room.

IN YOUR REFRIGERATOR

The inside of your refrigerator has a plastic lining and may have plastic shelves and drawers. Plastics are easy to wipe clean.

IN THE AIR

Airplanes are made of plastic. They used to be made of aluminum, but plastic weighs less, which makes the jets more fuel-efficient. That means they need less gas to get around.

ON YOUR HEAD

Your bike helmet is made from plastic. It's lightweight, strong, and keeps your precious head protected in case of a fall.

So, are all plastic products bad for the environment? Not necessarily. The items on this page can be reused over and over. They are much better for the environment than single-use plastics like straws, plastic utensils, and to-go containers. Turn to page 18 to learn more about single-use plastic.

THE PROBLEMS WITH PLASTIC

The first step in making a change is understanding why it needs to be changed in the first place.

PLASTIC IS TOO CONVENIENT!

PLASTIC - PROBLEM - #1

What do shopping bags, plastic cutlery, beverage bottles, takeaway cups, and straws have in common? They are all single-use plastics.

Single-use plastics are used once and then thrown away. They're lightweight, cheap, waterproof, disposable, strong—all the things that make plastic so convenient! Some, like coffee stir sticks, are used for just a few seconds before landing in a trash can.

About 40 percent of plastics are single-use plastics. That's a whole lotta plastic. But there's an even bigger problem: it takes *400 years* or more for many single-use plastics to degrade, or break down. Some plastic will *never* break down. So, you could spend a few minutes eating your lunch with a plastic fork, but then that fork might sit in a landfill for centuries. That math doesn't make sense, right?

SO WHY ARE WE STILL USING IT?

Plastic helps restaurants and businesses save time and money. Throwaway cups, plates, straws, and utensils don't have to be cleaned. It's just easier! But if we really want to change, we need to stop choosing convenience over everything else.

Replacing plastic takes a little more effort and sometimes it costs a bit more money. A paper straw costs a penny more than a plastic one. For big restaurant chains that need millions of straws every year, that's a lot of money! But the extra efforts won't go unnoticed by Mother Earth or future generations who will live on this planet.

NOW THAT'S PROGRESS!

Cities, countries, and companies around the world are banning single-use plastics, from bags to straws to silverware. The whole country of Canada has agreed to ban all single-use plastics by 2021. And the bans are making a big difference. In Australia, after two of the country's largest supermarket chains banned plastic shopping bags, the country used 80 percent fewer shopping bags within a few months. Amazing!

RECYCLING PLASTIC ISN'T EASY

"Reduce, reuse, recycle" is a common slogan used to encourage people to help the planet. But when it comes to plastic, "reduce, reuse, and *refuse*" is a better mantra.

The majority of plastic ends up in the garbage and the ocean. Only nine percent of all the plastic in the world has been recycled! (By contrast, more than 60 percent of paper is recycled in the U.S.)

How did that happen? Well, recycling is confusing. Certain plastics can be recycled. Others can't. And even those plastics that can be recycled often end up in the trash.

Unfortunately, once plastic gets mixed with colored dyes and other materials (like plastic toys often are) or tainted with food scraps (like food storage containers often are), it can't be recycled anymore. It's just too hard to separate the non-recyclable stuff from the recyclable stuff.

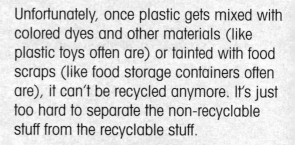

THE BIG PICTURE

Even if we put plastic in the recycling bin, we can't guarantee that it will end up at a recycling center. Plastic bags easily blow out of bins before or during the pick-up process. It's better to avoid plastic in the first place!

RECYCLING IS A BUSINESS!

The reality is that recycling isn't free. It takes a lot of people, time, effort, and money. Whatever you throw into your recycling bin gets picked up by a truck, sorted, broken down, and sold to another company that will turn it into a recycled product. That's how recycling centers make money.

In order to keep their recycled materials pure and clean, recycling centers have to stay very organized and focused. That means some items that are more difficult to recycle (like plastic bags, which can easily get caught up in and break recycling machines), can't be placed in recycling bins for pickup. Instead, families have to bring them to a special center. But, sadly, it's unlikely that people will go out of their way to recycle. Instead, those kinds of items often end up in the trash.

TOP COUNTRIES FOR RECYCLING

1. Germany
2. Austria
3. South Korea

WHAT HAPPENS TO PLASTIC IN THE TRASH?

Put a banana peel or cardboard scraps into a pile of dirt and it will eventually disappear. How? When something is biodegradable, it naturally breaks down into smaller and smaller pieces until it disappears into the soil.

Put plastic in a landfill and it could stick around for hundreds of years. Most plastic is not biodegradable, which means it's extra important that it makes it to the proper recycling center. Since the 1950s, we've created 8.3 billion metric tons of plastic. That's the same weight as 25,000 Empire State Buildings! And we aren't showing any signs of slowing down.

BANANA PEEL

3-5 WEEKS

MILK CARTON

5 YEARS

ALUMINUM CAN

80-200 YEARS

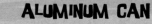

PLASTIC WATER BOTTLE

450-1,000 YEARS

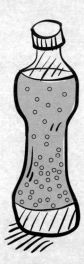

STYROFOAM CUP

500 YEARS TO FOREVER

THE BIG PICTURE

A landfill is a dedicated area where garbage is buried and covered with soil. Everything we place in a garbage bag eventually makes it to a landfill site. It's hard to guess how many landfills there are around the world. But we do know one thing: as more people populate the planet, the piles keep growing.

Bantar Gebang in Jakarta, Indonesia is one of the largest landfills in Asia. Recycling is not easily available there, so half of the area's plastic waste ends up in this dump and the rest ends up in the ocean. When landfills get full, they get shut down. Then another landfill has to be found somewhere else. One landfill outside of Los Angeles, California, is the size of New York City's Central Park.

PLASTIC IS POLLUTING OUR OCEANS

PROBLEM · PLASTIC · #3

If plastic doesn't end up at a recycling center and it doesn't end up in a landfill, where does it go? Often, the answer is the ocean. Tragically, our oceans have become the world's biggest garbage dump.

MILLIONS & MILLIONS OF TONS

All kinds of trash end up in the ocean including bottles, food containers, fishing nets, plastic bags, toothbrushes, and more. With 8 million tons of plastic going into our oceans each year, scientists estimate that there will be more than 150 million tons of plastic floating around by 2025.

OCEAN DUMPING ACT

For decades, New York City and many other cities around the world used to purposely dump their garbage directly in the ocean. A 1972 U.S. law nicknamed the Ocean Dumping Act helped put an end to this. But garbage from decades ago is probably still floating in the ocean today. And unfortunately, even more is joining it.

Any kind of garbage that ends up floating in the ocean is called "marine debris."

MOVING MARINE DEBRIS

It doesn't matter where marine debris is dumped. The Earth has just one big, connected ocean, and the waves are always moving. So, plastic from the other side of the world can float all the way around to your local beach.

Trash has been found in the Mariana Trench, which is the deepest spot in the ocean, as well as on Henderson Island, an island in the Pacific Ocean that has no people living on it!

SAVE THE SEA TURTLES (AND FRIENDS!)

By 2050, researchers believe there will be more plastic than fish in the world's ocean (by weight). What's even more alarming is the effect plastic has on fish, birds, and sea animals.

NOT OUR BAG!

More than 100,000 marine mammals die each year from plastic bags alone. Sea turtles mistake plastic bags for jellyfish, which is their favorite kind of food. It can get stuck in their stomachs and kill them. It's estimated that half of the world's sea turtles have accidentally eaten plastic.

STARVED BY PLASTIC

Dead whales have washed up on shore with as much as 88 pounds of plastic found in their stomachs, from bottles and caps to bags and straws. By 2050, scientists predict that plastic will be found in the stomachs of 99 percent of seabirds. They see floating objects and scoop them up in their beaks to feed to their babies. They just don't know any better. These kinds of animals end up starving because they believe their stomachs are full. Their bodies can't digest, or poop out, all of the plastic, so their stomachs never empty out.

No sea animal is safe. Seals, sea lions, whales, and dolphins all over the world have been hurt by plastic.

PLASTIC PAIN

Even if the plastic doesn't get eaten, it can negatively affect sea life. Plastic straws get stuck up the nostrils of sea turtles and cause them a lot of pain. Plastic balloon strings, fishing nets, and plastic six-pack rings can strangle them. Plastic bands can get stuck around fish or turtle shells, restricting their growth. Plastic bags can get attached to the fins of dolphins or get caught around a shark's gills.

CHANGE OUR HABITS

When plastic pollution enters the ocean, it disrupts the entire marine world. The best thing we can do right now is to avoid buying any new plastic where we can.

Check out the song "Turtle Ate a Jelly" by the Banana Slug String Band on their album *Only One Ocean*.

WHEN YOU HURT THE OCEAN, YOU HURT YOURSELF

Before Captain Charles Moore made an accidental discovery in 1997, we didn't realize how much plastic was entering our oceans. He told stories of the Great Pacific Garbage Patch, a huge floating collection of plastic trash.

This "plastic soup," as it's often called, swirls in the North Pacific Ocean between the west coast of the United States and Japan. It is believed to be twice the size of Texas or three times the size of France. About 1.8 trillion pieces of plastic can be found in it, which are estimated to weigh as much as 500 jumbo jets.

It's amazing that the Patch went undetected for so long. It can't be seen from high above because many of the plastics are so small that they are almost impossible to see. They're called "microplastics." Thanks to a combination of the sun, wind, and waves, some plastic breaks into tiny pieces, which turns the ocean into the cloudy plastic soup that it is today.

Microplastics are a huge problem because it's easy for fish to accidentally eat them. And then when we—and other marine mammals or birds—eat fish, we may be eating fish that have eaten these toxic microplastics. Which means we might be eating plastic or chemicals, too. Yuck! So, by polluting our oceans, we potentially pollute our own bodies.

1. North Pacific Gyre
2. Indian Ocean Gyre
3. South Pacific Gyre
4. South Atlantic Gyre
5. North Atlantic Gyre

There are now five known garbage patches in our seas that were formed by circulating ocean currents called gyres. Take a look at the map above to see them ranked in order of size.

PLANET PIONEER

In 2013, when he was 18 years old, Dutch inventor Boyan Slat vowed to find a solution to clean up the Great Pacific Garbage Patch. His floating net invention works with the ocean currents to help collect the trash. He believes a fleet of these floating systems will clean up half of the garbage patch within five years. Learn more at **www.theoceancleanup.com**.

PLASTIC IS HEATING UP THE PLANET

Plastic is made from petroleum. To get petroleum out of the Earth, workers drill deep into the ground or even into the ocean floor. It can then be turned into things like gasoline and plastic.

Petroleum is a fossil fuel. Fossil fuels run our cars, give our world electricity, and heat our homes. But fossil fuels aren't good for the environment because when they're burned for energy, they release gases into the air. Those gases trap heat from the sun in the same way that a greenhouse traps heat from the sun. That's why they're called greenhouse gases!

Plastic is made from petroleum (oil and natural gas), which costs less than other resources like paper or wood. That means that plastic is cheap! But that's not a good enough reason to continue to use it.

RISING TEMPERATURES

Earth is wrapped in a protective layer called an atmosphere. Every time we make more plastic cutlery or plastic bags, more gases are released. Then more gases get trapped under that layer and they collect more heat from the sun. Eventually the temperature of the planet increases a little bit at a time. And even more greenhouse gases get released when plastic naturally breaks down.

RISING SEA LEVELS

Even a slight increase in temperature can have devastating effects—for example, it can melt ice. If the polar ice caps melt, polar bears won't have a home. And the sea levels will rise, which could cause flooding along the shores. One thing leads to another, which leads to another!

NOW THAT'S PROGRESS!

There are more natural ways to create energy, such as by capturing energy produced by the sun or wind. These natural ways of creating energy are much cleaner than fossil fuels and they'll never run out. Fossil fuels are non-renewable sources, which means there's only a limited amount on Earth. Eventually, we'll run out of them. But we won't run out of sun or wind!

BIG IDEAS FOR A BETTER FUTURE

To really reduce our impact on the planet, we must
rethink many processes that we take for granted.
Together we have the power to break the cycle.
Get inspired by these creative solutions,
then dream up some of your own!

THE CIRCULAR ECONOMY

As humans, we make things and we buy things. (That's the basic definition of an economy.) But if we want to make a difference to the health of our planet, we must change how our economy works.

The way we make and buy things today is linear—that means it follows a straight line. Something is made, then bought, then used, then thrown away. The end. A circular economy is different. It changes the way we make and buy things from a straight line into a circle that continuously loops around and around. Something is made, bought, used, and then re-made into another product.

The most important part of the circular economy is that there is no waste. Things are designed to be used again and again instead of ending up in the garbage. The item could be simply reused, repurposed in a new way, or recycled into a totally new product.

When you recycle one product and turn it into another useful product it's called "upcycling."

PLANET PIONEER

Preserve is a company that has been making toothbrushes, plates, silverware, cups, and more from recycled plastic since 1996. When you're done using one of their products, you can send it back to them. They'll recycle it and create more products that get sold back to you again. Now that's a circular economy! **www.preserve.eco**

TAKE ACTION!

You can support the circular economy by buying recycled products. When you support companies that sell recycled materials, you are saying, "Hey, keep doing what you're doing!"

Another way to make your life more "circular" is to buy or borrow secondhand clothing, books, toys, and sports gear. And to take better care of the things you own so they last longer. When you give something a new life or a longer life, you prevent it from ending up in a landfill.

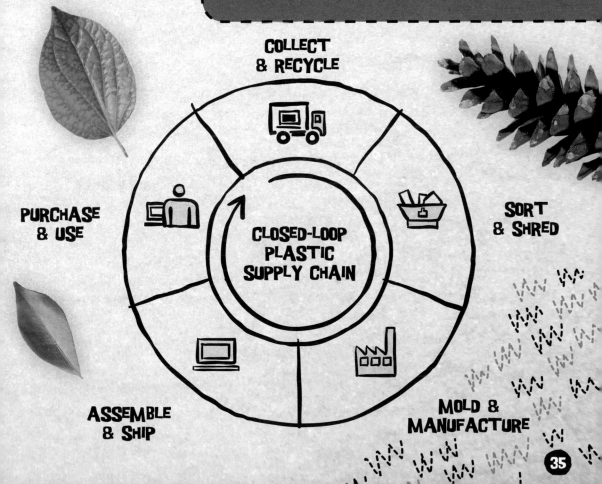

COLLECT
& RECYCLE

PURCHASE
& USE

CLOSED-LOOP
PLASTIC
SUPPLY CHAIN

SORT
& SHRED

ASSEMBLE
& SHIP

MOLD &
MANUFACTURE

THE ZERO WASTE MOVEMENT

Surely it's not possible to throw literally *nothing* away, is it?! Let's figure out what the zero waste movement is all about.

Imagine you brought a lunch to school in a cotton bag with metal silverware and a fabric napkin, a reusable water bottle, and just the right amount of food kept in aluminum containers. When you left the cafeteria, you'd have no trash to throw away. No recycling either. That's the zero waste movement!

Zero waste experts, including one woman named Kathryn Kellogg, can fit two years of trash into a single 16-ounce jar. How do they do it? They refuse, reduce, reuse, compost, and recycle! Learn how your family can follow some of these rules:

Refuse to buy things that come wrapped in a lot of packaging. That means eating fresh fruits and vegetables instead of buying things like chips and crackers that come in plastic wrap and boxes.

Do you really need that? That's one question you'll have to ask yourself if you're following the zero waste lifestyle. **Reduce** your environmental footprint by buying less stuff.

Reuse by taking care of your stuff, buying secondhand items when you can, and investing in reusable products like fabric food pouches, glass containers, and steel water bottles.

Instead of throwing food in the garbage, **compost** food scraps like fruits, vegetables, coffee grounds, and eggshells. (Paper, dryer lint, and cotton can be composted, too!) These items can be added to a special composting container. This container will then be picked up by a composting service, which may be free in your city. Or, there may be a drop-off location. Check your city's website to learn about your options. The composted material then gets used as fertilizer—which is good for the soil and helps reduce the amount of items in landfills.

If you do need to buy something, make sure you can recycle it! But **recycling** isn't the best solution. It's better to avoid plastic in the first place!

"PRECYCLING"

Precycling means choosing what's better for the environment instead of what's easier or more convenient. It means avoiding waste before it's even created!

You and your family members need things like groceries, clothing, and school supplies. Families around the world shop for these things every day! But if we want to change our planet for the better, we have to first change our actions for the better. That means making smarter choices when it comes to which products we use every day. One way to do that is by "precycling"!

You can encourage your whole family to get involved and buy products that are easier to recycle instead of purchasing products that you know will create a lot of trash. It means planning ahead and taking some extra time to be more considerate of the environment.

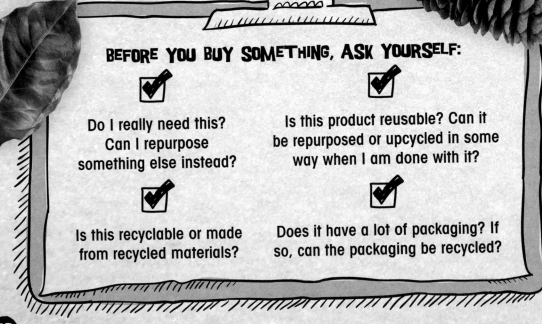

BEFORE YOU BUY SOMETHING, ASK YOURSELF:

☑ Do I really need this? Can I repurpose something else instead?

☑ Is this product reusable? Can it be repurposed or upcycled in some way when I am done with it?

☑ Is this recyclable or made from recycled materials?

☑ Does it have a lot of packaging? If so, can the packaging be recycled?

IS THERE A REPLACEMENT FOR PLASTIC?

Many inventors are trying to create alternatives to plastic. Replacements need to be waterproof, strong, lightweight, and moldable into many shapes. Here are a few that have been tried:

CORN

Plant-based plastics, also called bioplastics, are made from things like corn that can easily be grown.

STONE PAPER

Stone paper is made from crushed stones and can be used for packaging. It's recyclable and waterproof.

MUSHROOM

Mushroom-based packaging is grown in a week and takes a week to decompose. It's a good replacement for Styrofoam packaging.

WHAT ARE INVENTORS LOOKING FOR IN A PLASTIC REPLACEMENT?

SOMETHING THAT'S RENEWABLE

A renewable resource is something that comes from nature that can be replaced once it's used. Forests are one example—trees can be cut down to make paper, but more trees can be planted easily.

ECO CHALLENGE!

Is there one plastic item you or your family can give up this week? What can you replace it with that's better for the environment?

SOMETHING THAT'S REUSABLE

Reusable and recyclable can go hand in hand. But it's not just about being recycled once. Can it be recycled over and over again so it can make more and more products? Or is it strong enough to be used hundreds of times?

SOMETHING THAT'S NON-TOXIC

We don't want poisonous substances entering our body or our environment. Plastic items often touch our food and water. Replacements can't be harmful or poisonous.

The average American will use 38,000 straws between the ages of five and 65. If you said no to straws from now on, that's a lot of plastic that *won't* end up in the ocean. Each time you avoid plastic, you are saying, "I'm a guardian of this planet, and I'm going to make a better choice."

Moving forward, the goal is to add less *new* plastic in your life. If you own something that's plastic and it's reusable, keep using it until it needs to be replaced. At that time, you can choose something that's better for the environment.

TAKE ACTION!

Learn how to become a plastic patroller—someone who avoids plastic—instead of a plastic polluter! Avoiding plastic takes a lot of effort. And you may wonder if that effort will make a difference. We promise that it will!

IN YOUR BEDROOM

Right now your room is probably filled with plastic—but it doesn't have to be. Here are some simple ideas for more environmentally friendly alternatives. Take a look!

1 TRY TO AVOID PLASTIC TOYS

Saving up your allowance for something special? Making a birthday gift wish list? Next time think twice about what toys you really want. Plastic toys are terrible for the environment. Instead, choose toys that are made from earth-friendlier materials like wood, metal, natural rubber, cotton, paper, or recycled plastic.

2 BUY USED TOYS OR BORROW THEM

If there's a plastic toy you really have your sights set on, see if you can buy it secondhand. An adult can help you find what you're looking for at a resale shop, yard sale, or online message board. Or maybe you can borrow it from a friend!

3 OPT FOR EXPERIENCES INSTEAD OF TOYS

Cutting down on the number of toys you own is better for the environment. Instead of asking for or gifting plastic toys every birthday and holiday, consider experiences instead. Here are some gift ideas to give or ask for:

Gift card to an ice cream shop

A membership to a zoo or aquarium

Tickets to a show, concert, or musical

Passes to a theme park or museum

Gift certificate for movie tickets and popcorn

Supplies or equipment for a hobby

THE BIG PICTURE

Toys used to be made of wood or metal. But around 1940, toy companies learned they could save money by making toys with a new cheap material called plastic. Now 90 percent of toys are made from it.

This is a huge problem for the planet. Plastic toys often can't be recycled because they're made of different kinds of plastic that have been mixed together, colored, and attached to other materials like metal. It's too expensive to separate those materials from one another and recycle them individually.

That leaves one option: plastic toys end up in the trash. The plastic toys sitting in your room will eventually sit in a landfill until you're as old as your grandparents—or longer!

4 DONATE YOUR TOYS

How many of your toys do you still play with? There may be more than a few that you've outgrown. Another kid could have a lot of fun with them! Instead of throwing them in the garbage, pass them along to someone else. Here are some local places that may be looking for toys…

Daycare center

Library

Homeless shelter for children

After-school program

Resale shop

5 ORGANIZE A TOY SWAP

Here is a fun way to get yourself some new toys without paying a penny or creating any waste. Just gather up some of your unwanted toys and invite over your friends. Don't forget to ask them to bring along some of their toys to swap, too. The best thing about this is everyone ends up with new toys and it's completely free. Everyone is a winner! You could also look for toy libraries in your area.

NOW THAT'S PROGRESS!

Some of the most popular toys in the world are made from plastic, including LEGO® bricks and Barbies. And that's a problem. But some companies are making changes for the better. By 2030, LEGO® hopes that all of their petroleum-based plastic bricks will be made from plant-based or recycled materials. They'll still look and work the same, but will be better for Planet Earth. That's great news!

6 REFUSE FAST FOOD TOYS

Fast food chains often give away plastic toys as part of their kids' meals. Many people think these are wasteful and should be banned. How about saying no to your next free toy? If everyone did this, it would make a big statement and perhaps encourage companies to change. They could switch the material of their toys to something less environmentally harmful or give away something other than toys, like small books!

IN YOUR CLOSET

There are many ways you can be kinder to the environment with your clothing choices. Here are some handy hints to help you.

7 ## TAKE CARE OF YOUR CLOTHING

When you take better care of the stuff you own, it lasts longer. When we use what we have—and make it last as long as we can—that's good for the environment. We buy less and throw less away. Even if you stain or rip a shirt, ask an adult to help you clean it or repair it. The faster you do so, the sooner you can wear it again.

Organize a clothing swap with your friends or the kids in your neighborhood. Ask everyone to bring five clean items of clothing. Arrange and display all of the donated items nicely on a table. Then take turns "shopping" for pieces. You can do this with toys, too!

8 ## GET EXCITED ABOUT HAND-ME-DOWNS

Don't let the sound of hand-me-downs make you grumble. Just think, it's the chance to have a whole new wardrobe without having to shop. You can try out a new style that you might not usually go for. Have you got any cool older cousins? Let them know that you'll be first in line when they grow out of their wardrobe!

9 WEAR COTTON

Much of our clothing is made from synthetic fibers that eventually pollute our oceans. Ask your family to consider shopping for clothing made from 100-percent natural fibers like organic cotton (which is pesticide-free), linen, and hemp whenever possible.

10 CHOOSE SECONDHAND

Secondhand clothing is a great way to get more use out of perfectly good clothing. And like we already mentioned, that's a great thing! Whether you get them online or at a resale shop, there are lots of fab finds at good prices. Some of the items may have only been worn once or twice, if at all, so they still have plenty of wear in them.

THE BIG PICTURE

Every time your clothing gets washed, the ocean gets polluted. How?

About 60 percent of clothing worldwide is made out of plastic—synthetic materials like nylon, polyester, and acrylic. Each time you run a load of laundry, hundreds of thousands of teeny-tiny plastic fibers fall off the clothing and into the water.

That same water eventually makes it to the sewage treatment plant. The treated wastewater is often dumped back into rivers or the ocean—and so are the shreds of plastic. That pollution is called microplastics and, as we know, microplastics can pollute our oceans, get eaten by marine animals and show up in the cooked fish we eat for dinner.

Microplastics can even fall off your clothing while you're walking around. They're so small that you wouldn't even notice!

RECYCLE YOUR WORN-OUT ATHLETIC SHOES

Don't throw away that smelly old pair of sneakers. Did you know trainers can be turned into playgrounds, running tracks and basketball courts? It's true! Most Nike stores around the world will collect your old gym shoes—they don't have to be Nike brand—and recycle them. Your tennis shoes will get turned into sports surfaces or into new shoes and clothing.

You can also mail your shoes directly to Nike's Reuse-A-Shoe program:

Nike Recycling Center

26755 SW 95th Ave.

Wilsonville, OR 97070

USA

If your shoes are in good condition but you've simply outgrown them, consider donating them to a resale organization or handing them down to a friend or sibling who can use them.

ECO CHALLENGE!

Count all the plastic items in your room right now. Don't forget your closet and inside your backpack!

PLANET PIONEER

Many sporting apparel companies that usually use a lot of plastic-based materials for shoes and clothing have changed directions for the better. Nike has been recycling shoes since 1992. Now 75 percent of all Nike shoes and clothing are made from some sort of recycled material. Adidas plans to use only recycled plastic in all of its shoes and sporting apparel by 2024. And Patagonia has been making clothing from materials like organic cotton, recycled soda bottles, and natural rubber since the 1970s. One way to make a difference is to buy things from companies who care about the environment. It shows that you care about the environment and it encourages companies to keep caring for the environment, too!

12 DON'T CHUCK BROKEN JEWELRY

If you don't know what to do with your old, broken, and unwanted jewelry, don't throw it into the garbage. Broken accessories like watches, necklace chains, or odd earrings can be recycled. Just do a bit of research online with a grown-up to find out about the most convenient place for you to do this. Some charities accept damaged jewelry to raise money for good causes.

IN THE BATHROOM

This is one of the worst places in your home when it comes to plastic. From shampoo bottles to toothpaste and brushes, it's everywhere!

13 CHOOSE A BETTER TOOTHBRUSH

You need to brush your teeth. And your toothbrushes should be replaced every few months. That means you could easily use more than 300 toothbrushes over the course of your life!

If they're made from plastic, that would be 300 toothbrushes added to the trash. Toothbrushes aren't easy to recycle because they're made of a few different materials—nylon bristles, plastic handles, and metal staples. Those materials need to be separated before they can be recycled, which makes recycling even more expensive.

One way to minimize the amount of waste you create while keeping your teeth clean is to buy a toothbrush made from bamboo or recycled materials. Or buy an electric toothbrush with a replaceable head. That means you'll change the bristles every few months, but you can use the handle over and over again.

Visit a health food or natural beauty store, or ask an adult to help you look online for one of these products.

14 FORGET THE TOOTHPASTE TUBE

Squeezable toothpaste tubes are really hard to recycle. One way to address this problem is to avoid them. Hang on though, this doesn't mean you have permission to stop brushing your teeth!

One alternative is tooth powders. These often come in an easy-to-recycle container that holds a lot more than a typical toothpaste tube. That means less waste over time. You simply pour a tiny bit of powder into your palm, wet your toothbrush and dip it in the powder. They're often made with natural ingredients—and studies have found that they clean even better than toothpaste.

Another option is to chew your way to clean teeth with toothpaste tablets. They look like candy but are anything but. Pop one in your mouth with a bit of water, chew, and then brush with the paste you've created.

15 SIGN UP FOR A RECYCLING PROGRAM

TerraCycle partners with big companies around the world, like Colgate, to help collect hard-to-recycle products. When you sign up for their program, they'll mail you an envelope for items like your toothpaste tubes or toothbrushes. Send them back and TerraCycle will take care of the recycling! Learn more at **www.terracycle.com**.

16 BUY BIGGER BOTTLES

What's better for the environment: three small plastic bottles or one big one? One big one is right! If your family prefers to use shower products in plastic bottles, opt for bulk-sized bottles that can be used for months instead of smaller bottles that may need to be replaced every few weeks. It's not a perfect fix, but it is a better option!

17 CLEAN YOUR EARS WITH A CLOTH

Cotton swabs (or cotton buds) are two wads of cotton attached to the ends of a stick. Sometimes the stick is made of paper, but other times it's made from plastic. They get used once then get thrown away. Some people even flush them down the toilet where they eventually end up in the ocean. No good! Instead of using a swab (which is dangerous to stick inside your ear anyway), simply use a washcloth to wipe the insides of your ear the next time you shower or bathe.

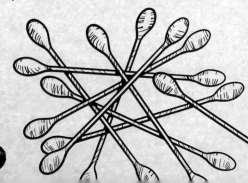

NOW THAT'S PROGRESS!

In England, cotton buds (as well as plastic straws and drink stirrers) are going to be banned. That'll save an estimated 2 billion plastic-stemmed cotton buds from ending up in landfills every year. Great news!

NOW THAT'S PROGRESS!

Instead of giving away tiny plastic shampoo and conditioner bottles, in 2019 some hotel chains like Marriott switched to using larger, refillable containers that are mounted to the walls. Those containers hold a lot more product and can be used over and over again instead of creating waste every day.

18 ADD A RECYCLING BIN TO YOUR BATHROOM

You likely have a small garbage can in your bathroom—but where does all the recycling go? So many plastic-wrapped or plastic-based products can be found in the bathroom. Think about disposable contact lenses and the cases they come in, or dental floss and the container it comes in! It's all plastic.

And it often ends up in the trash. By adding a second small bin to your bathroom, you can help make sure more of the recyclables make it to the recycling center. Or search for a small split waste bin online that has two compartments—one for garbage and one for recycling.

19 SWITCH TO BARS OF SOAP

Solid soap bars are much better for the environment than liquid soaps, which come in plastic bottles. Replacing your body wash and hand wash with a bar of soap is a quick and easy fix. Another benefit of bars is that they last longer than the bottles do—two to three times longer. That means less waste!

There are probably even more things in your bathroom that are made from plastic—like your shower curtain, dental floss, hair brush, bandages, and more. Once these items are worn out or used up, you can find non-plastic replacements for them and all the plastic products mentioned in this section online or at health food and natural beauty stores.

THE BIG PICTURE

Products are usually made at one location but then have to be shipped to stores across the country or around the world via boat, plane, train, or truck. When things are larger and heavier, fewer of them can be transported at one time. And each time something is transported, pollution is created.

Think of a bar of soap compared to a bottle of liquid soap. A bar of soap and the packaging surrounding it is very small and lightweight. That means more can be transported at one time, which means less pollution. So, by choosing a bar of soap over a bottle, you're creating less trash *and* less pollution. Sometimes these small changes have a bigger impact than we think!

20 USE SOLID BODY PRODUCTS

Trade in your shampoo bottle for a bar!
These plastic-free alternatives come in
heaps of colors and scents, and there
are different ones to suit most hair types.
You can also find solid alternatives for
conditioner, body lotion, and more! These
simple swaps are easy now that so many
companies are dedicated to reducing
plastic waste and are producing solid
toiletry options.

CONDITIONER
BAR

LOTION
BAR

SHAMPOO
BAR

21 VISIT ZERO WASTE STORES

Did you know that there are stores where
you can refill your empty toiletry bottles?
It's true. Look out for one near you to find
out exactly what they offer. Some allow you
to take along your empty dish soap and
laundry liquid containers to refill them with
eco-friendly products. This is a great way
to get the most out of the plastic bottles
you already have.

MAKE DIY BATH BOMBS

These fun and fizzy bath bomb creations are easy to create and they make awesome gifts for your friends and family.

Remember to store them somewhere dry and use them up within a couple of weeks or they won't fizz anymore!

YOU WILL NEED:

½ cup cream of tartar

2 cups baking soda

1 tsp food coloring

2 tsp food flavoring

A tiny splash of water

Glass mixing bowl

Rubber gloves

Spoon

Cookie trays for molds

MAKE IT!

DIRECTIONS

1. First, put on the gloves. Use your hands to mix up the cream of tartar with the baking soda in your bowl.

2. Drop in the food coloring and flavoring—yellow and lemon make a good combination—and mix well.

3. Add a tiny splash of water to your mixture. The mixture should be crumbly and just hold its shape.

4. Carefully pack the mixture tightly into your molds using a spoon.

5. Now leave this to dry for 24 hours.

6. When completely dry, pop them out of the molds. You can wrap them in paper and give them to friends as gifts.

AT LUNCH

School cafeterias create a lot of waste, but you can easily help reduce the amount your school makes. Here are some simple changes that we can all try out.

23 REPLACE YOUR SQUEEZABLE SNACK AND JUICE POUCHES

Look around the cafeteria or canteen at your school, and you'll see them everywhere! But each squeezable snack and juice pouch is destined for the dump. Because they're made of different plastics and aluminum fused together, snack pouches and juice pouches can't easily be recycled, reused, or composted. It's better to eat yogurt or applesauce out of a glass or recyclable tub and juice out of a box or bottle.

24 SWITCH TO REUSABLE ZIP BAGS AND LUNCHBOX CONTAINERS

If you bring a lunch to school, forget the plastic zip-top bags. Replace them with reusable plastic or silicone zip-top pouches or with reusable containers, which can be made from plastic, metal, or glass. (Reusable plastic packaging is better than non-reusable packaging!) But also consider pouches made from fabric, which is washable, reusable, and perfect for storing snacks. Or get creative and wrap your sandwich in a bandana—bonus: it doubles as a napkin!

You can find reusable plastic, silicone, or fabric pouches and containers at craft fairs or kitchen goods stores as well as online or through websites like **www.etsy.com** that sell homemade items.

THE BIG PICTURE

Stand up pouches look nice when they sit on a shelf at a grocery store. They are lightweight and are easy to use. That's why so many companies choose them for baby food, coffee, yogurt, juice, laundry detergent, and more. But they're really hard to recycle and won't be picked up by your curbside recycling program. Until companies decide to stop using them—and consumers decide to stop buying them—they'll continue to sit in landfills around the world.

25 MAKE HOMEMADE SINGLE PORTIONS

Chip bags can't be recycled. They are made from many types of materials, which are hard to separate and recycle. So, when it comes to individually-wrapped snack packs—that's a lot of garbage! Instead of buying small packs of personal-sized chips, crackers, or pretzels for lunch, make your own single servings from a large bulk bag instead. Help prepare your lunch by portioning a handful of snacks into reusable packaging, like a fabric or reusable plastic pouch.

26 RECYCLE PROPERLY

Learn the recycling rules for your community by visiting the website of your city's recycling program. The better you are at following the rules, the more successful your city's recycling program will be! Find out which plastics they accept. Do they accept thin plastic film or unusual items like balloons? Or is it better for those to be thrown in the trash? Every city has different rules, but what's most important is that you follow them when you're at school, home, or anywhere else.

Whenever you can, rinse recyclable plastic or glass items with water to completely remove juice, yogurt, or any other food residue.

TerraCycle will take certain kinds of snack pouches and chip bags and recycle them. Visit **www.terracycle.com** for more info.

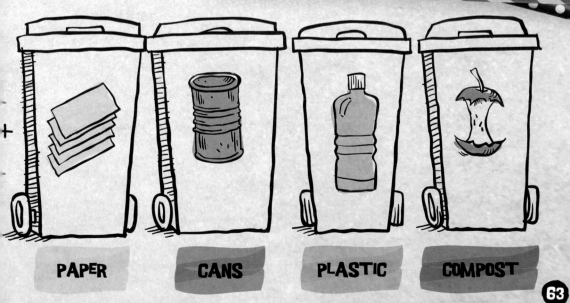

PAPER   CANS   PLASTIC   COMPOST

27 DITCH PLASTIC CUTLERY

It's easy to grab a plastic fork or spoon from the cafeteria or from a restaurant. But we know that this kind of single-use plastic is so terrible for the environment—and easy to avoid. Petition your school lunchroom to offer biodegradable bamboo cutlery. Maybe they'd even consider switching to metal silverware that can be washed and reused! Ask your teacher and your classmates for help in organizing a campaign to make a change at your school.

If you do want to chew, look for biodegradable gum that's free from plastics. You can find it at health food stores or online.

28 GIVE UP GUM!

Bet you never knew there was plastic in your chewing gum! Plastic helps create a long-lasting chew and flavorful gum base. It's not bad for you, but once you spit it out, it's bad for the environment. Chewing gum gets littered all over planet—both inside and outside. It won't biodegrade, and it's very difficult and expensive to recycle. And what's the point of gum anyway? It doesn't have any health benefits for you, so you might as well quit!

Around the world, 374 trillion pieces of gum are sold each year, which would take 187 billion hours to chew if each piece was chewed for 30 minutes.

OUT TO EAT

You can make a difference outside your home, too, just by refusing disposable straws or takeaway cups. Making small changes like these can have a big long-term impact!

29 SIP FROM THE SIDE!

In a single day in the United States, it's estimated that 500 million plastic straws are used. Straws are one example of single-use plastic—that's plastic that gets used once and often for only a very short amount of time. Then it ends up in a landfill or in the ocean for decades and decades. Instead of grabbing a plastic straw, sip your drink without one. You don't need it!

NOW THAT'S PROGRESS!

The fight against straws is growing around the world. Restaurants, hotel chains, airlines, amusement parks, and more have agreed to phase out plastic straws. The list includes Starbucks, the Walt Disney Company, McDonald's, SeaWorld Entertainment, and Pret A Manger among many others.

PASS ON PLASTIC TO-GO LIDS

30

When you opt to sip from the side instead of using a straw, you'll find that you don't need that plastic lid either, especially if you're eating in at a restaurant. That's great because plastic lids are also terrible for the environment. By giving up both the lid and the straw, you're making a huge difference. Go, you!

If you really need a straw, choose a paper straw or reusable metal one instead. You can carry a reusable metal straw with you just like you would carry a reusable water bottle or reusable silverware. It's these little changes that will make a big impact!

PLANET PIONEER

Thankfully there are alternatives to plastic straws like metal, paper, and pasta—yes, pasta! The Amazing Pasta Straw was created by Bob Morris, who owns an ocean-front restaurant in Malibu, California. He saw firsthand how much pollution goes into the ocean as well as how many of his customers used straws once and threw them away. So, he turned a long, thick dried pasta noodle with a hollow center into a straw. It's the perfect way to sip, and it doesn't disintegrate quickly like paper does. Now that's a smart way to sip!

31 ORDER THE CONE INSTEAD OF THE CUP

Imagine some kind of device that served food but then could be eaten afterward so it was zero waste. It has already been invented—it's called the ice cream cone! Paper cups or bowls might seem harmless, but they're often lined with a plastic coating, which makes them difficult to recycle. Either way, whenever you have the option to go waste-free, you should choose it. So, say yes to the cone!

32 BE PROACTIVE AND SAY, "NO, THANK YOU!" TO TAKEAWAY CUTLERY

Does your family ever order dinner in? If you order a meal for delivery or pick up, it often comes with a plastic-wrapped napkin and silverware set. But if you're eating at home, you don't need this stuff! Ask an adult to say, "We don't need silverware or napkins," when they place an order. Here's another tip: if you know you'll be eating at a restaurant that only has plastic silverware, bring your own reusable set in a container. You can find them at camping supply stores.

33 FORGO THE TO-GO CONTAINER

When you order food to go at a restaurant, you're bound to end up with plastic take-out containers. They're often made of Styrofoam or another single-use plastic, can't be recycled, and often come in a plastic bag! Ask the restaurant if they offer cardboard containers instead. Or consider bringing along a glass container that can be filled with food and a reusable bag to carry away your order. If that's not an option, dining inside the restaurant is way better for the environment.

34 DON'T GRAB SINGLE-SERVE ITEMS

When you have the opportunity, put a condiment directly onto your plate instead of in a tiny plastic container. And don't grab single-sized serving packets of ketchup or mustard if you know there are bottles sitting on the table at the restaurant or sitting in your refrigerator at home, which is where you are headed to eat. These single servings are convenient for a short moment, but they can affect our environment for a lifetime.

35 KEEP FOOD OUT OF THE RECYCLING BIN

A lot of garbage accidentally ends up in recycling bins. That's because people are confused by what can and can't be recycled. This can lead to contamination—that means perfectly good recyclables get stained or ruined by food and have to be sent to the trash instead.

So, remember this one easy recycling rule: no food in the recycling can! That means no food scraps, things that are stained with food remains, or liquids. Even if a plate or cup is recyclable, it's not recyclable if it's covered with food. It has to be thrown into the trash can. When you keep food out of the recycling bin, you ensure that more things can be recycled!

PLANET PIONEER

Recycling is confusing! There are slightly different rules for every city, state, and country. But signs can help. Sadly, there isn't universal signage that clearly and easily states the rules so that people can recycle properly at home, schools, stores, and restaurants.

When people know what goes where, it can reduce the amount of trash and increase the amount of recycling all over the world. Recycle Across America is an organization that wants to increase recycling by creating better labels. If the instructions are easier to understand then people can recycle the right way.

Visit **www.recycleacrossamerica.org** for more information on how simple recycling signs can make a big difference at schools, offices, and restaurants. Even if you don't live in the United States, you can learn some tips!

36 ASK FOR A CHANGE

Next time you're at a local restaurant, cafe, or your own school cafeteria, look around and see how much plastic waste is being created. If you see a lot, speak up! Tell someone behind the cash register, a server, a teacher, or a manager why plastic is bad. Ask if they'd be willing to make some changes that are better for the environment. Here are some ideas:

☑ Provide reusable cups.

☑ Replace plastic stirrers with cardboard ones.

☑ Replace plastic straws with paper ones.

☑ Provide a discount if you bring your own cup.

☑ Only give straws when asked.

☑ Stop providing plastic bags for takeout.

Switch takeout containers to a compostable container.

Stop providing single-serve condiments.

Add a recycling bin if they don't already have one.

Don't provide plastic silverware or dishes.

Label recycling bins and garbage cans more clearly.

Move the recycling bin so it's easier to see.

AT THE GROCERY STORE

You and your family can make a big difference every time you step foot in a supermarket. Here are a few ways that you can reduce your impact on the environment.

37 BRING YOUR OWN REUSABLE BAG

There are no ifs, ands, or buts about it—plastic bags are bad for the environment. Some estimates have found that 500 billion plastic bags are used each year globally, which amounts to about 150 bags for each person who lives on Earth. And they're typically used for only 12 minutes before they're thrown away.

Plastic bags aren't easy to recycle, which means they end up in a landfill or the ocean—and could take hundreds of years to decompose. Always have a reusable bag on hand when you leave the house! So you don't forget, keep one stored near the front door or in the backseat of your car. There are many small foldable bags that can easily fit in your backpack or in a parent's carryall.

The best kind of reusable bag is a fabric one. The cheap reusable bags that are sold at stores are often made from plastic. Plus, fabric can be easily washed, which is important when you're carrying food in these bags.

NOW THAT'S PROGRESS!

People all over the world know that plastic bags are a big problem. In 2002, Bangladesh became the first country to ban plastic bags. Now more countries have followed, including China, France, and New Zealand. Some of these bans are very serious. For example, if you make, sell, or use a plastic bag in Kenya, you'll be fined $40,000 or jailed for four years!

In the United States, only a small handful of states (California, Hawaii, and New York) have a plastic bag ban. Hopefully more will follow! Some states have added a tax on plastic bags to discourage people from using them. Denmark was the first country to do this in 1993. Now people in Denmark use only about four plastic bags per year, which is much better than Americans, who average one bag per day.

Plastic bags are one of the most common kinds of trash found floating in the ocean. These bags get eaten by sea birds and other marine mammals that mistake them for food. This can cause animals to get sick and die.

Of the million plastic bags used each minute globally, only one in 200 will be recycled. According to some scientists, unrecycled bags can take up to 1,000 years to decompose.

38 SKIP THE PRODUCE BAGS

When your family heads to the grocery store, don't put every piece of produce in a plastic bag. It's ok if they roll around your cart or basket. Just wash them off when you get home! Or, bring some reusable mesh bags or fabric bags that hold your produce while your family shops.

ECO CHALLENGE!

Make your next trip to the grocery store a family affair. Divide up the shopping list, then challenge everyone to gather items with as little plastic as possible.

PLANET PIONEER

Zero waste grocery stores around the world have vowed to make a difference in reducing plastic pollution. That means selling food without packaging. Customers have to bring in their own containers and can scoop out the exact amount they need whether it's pasta, cereal, or beans. Other stores have added plastic-free aisles, like Ekoplaza in Amsterdam. In 2018, they unveiled an aisle filled with 700 products, from meat to cereal to yogurt to snacks, that are free of plastic packaging.

39 BUY IN BULK

Ask your family to buy things like oatmeal, granola, cereal, nuts, and beans from the bulk aisle. That means you'll scoop exactly what you need into a bag (hopefully you've brought a reusable one!). This is better for the environment because there's no packaging—and that means no garbage.

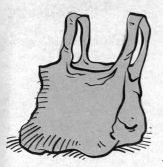

Speaking of bags, don't put your recycling in a plastic garbage bag! Garbage bags can get caught in sorting machines just as easily as plastic shopping bags.

40 RECYCLE PLASTIC BAGS PROPERLY

If you do use a plastic bag, be sure to follow the rules about how to recycle it the right way. Shopping bags are mostly made from #2 plastic while thinner produce bags are made from #4 (see pages 8-11 for a reminder of the different types of plastic). Both are recyclable, but there might be a special place you have to drop them off in order to recycle them.

If your city's recycling program doesn't accept plastic bags, don't throw them into your at-home recycling bin—they won't get recycled that way. Plus, they can too easily get caught in the machines at your local recycling center and cause it to break down, which is no good. In the end, it will just get sent to a landfill.

First, decide if you can reuse the plastic bags a few more times. Some plastic bags are meant to be reused again and again! If you can't reuse it, collect bags over a period of time and then bring them to a nearby plastic bag recycling program. Grocery stores often have recycling bins for plastic bags.

THE BIG PICTURE

Are paper bags better than plastic? Yes, but… the reality is that any disposable item has a negative effect on the environment. It takes a lot of water, energy, and resources to make paper bags. The best choice will always be to bring your own reusable item instead of choosing a plastic or paper one, whether it's a bag, plate, or cup.

PAY ATTENTION TO PACKAGING

Think about all of your favorite foods at the grocery store. What kind of packaging do they come in? Some items at the grocery store have way more packaging than they need. For example, you might find fruit pre-cut into cubes and sold in a plastic tub. Or a vegetable medley placed on a foam tray with plastic around it. Or frozen broccoli in plastic bags in the refrigerated section. Instead, consider grabbing the fresh produce with no wrapping. You'll be making a much better choice for the environment.

The majority of plastic products made today are plastic packaging, which is used for less than six months before it ends up in a landfill.

THE BIG PICTURE

Plastic film is one of the worst kinds of single-use plastic. It's used for wrapping around bread, bottled water cases, napkins, toilet paper, and paper plates. Because it may not be recycled by your community's curbside program, you may not be able to throw it into your own recycling bin. But you can collect it and bring it somewhere special to be recycled—the same places you can bring plastic bags. Head to **www.plasticfilmrecycling.org** to find a drop-off location in the United States or Canada.

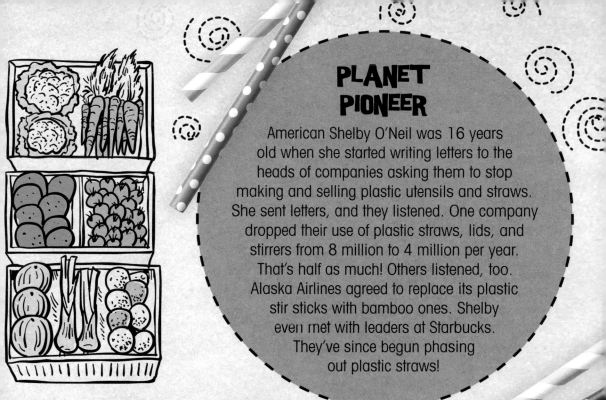

PLANET PIONEER

American Shelby O'Neil was 16 years old when she started writing letters to the heads of companies asking them to stop making and selling plastic utensils and straws. She sent letters, and they listened. One company dropped their use of plastic straws, lids, and stirrers from 8 million to 4 million per year. That's half as much! Others listened, too. Alaska Airlines agreed to replace its plastic stir sticks with bamboo ones. Shelby even met with leaders at Starbucks. They've since begun phasing out plastic straws!

42 PUT PRESSURE ON WASTEFUL COMPANIES

Have you seen a food product in a grocery store that has a lot of unnecessary and harmful plastic packaging? Did it make you mad? Do something about it! Customers shouldn't be fully responsible for caring for the planet—companies should be considering the environment, too!

Write a letter or an email to the company who makes that product. You can often find the name of the company and sometimes even the address printed right on the box or bag. Let them know why their packaging is bad and how they could change it.

43 THINK TWICE ABOUT BOTTLED WATER

Bottled water sure is convenient! Around the world, one million plastic bottles are bought each minute. That's a scary number. When you consider that 91% of all plastic never gets recycled, that means plastic bottles end up in landfills or the ocean. And it can take 450 years for them to decompose.

Here's the good news: plastic bottles are an easy habit to break. Carrying around a reusable water bottle, like one made from aluminum, and filling up at water fountains or filtered water from the sink is a small habit that will make a huge difference. Seriously, a HUGE one! Plus, they come in fun colors and patterns. What's not to love?

For your own health, remember that a disposable plastic water bottle should never be used more than once!

THE BIG PICTURE

If plastic bottles can be recycled, what's the big deal? Recycling isn't the best solution—in fact, it should be the *last* solution. That's because when a plastic bottle gets recycled, it doesn't get turned into another plastic bottle. The material is very thin, so it's "downcycled" into a plastic fiber that can be turned into carpeting, clothing, or decking. (Downcycling is when a higher value product is turned into a lower value product. In this case, a bottle is turned into yarn.) This means that new plastic has to be created every time a plastic bottle is made. It's better to just avoid plastic in the first place.

FILTER YOUR WATER WITHOUT PLASTIC

Many people use plastic water pitchers containing a plastic filter. But there's an alternative: you can simply drop a stick of activated charcoal into a glass pitcher. Six to eight hours later, your water will be filtered. And the sticks last for three to four months! Activated charcoal sticks can be found online.

NOW THAT'S PROGRESS!

Organizers at the 2019 London Marathon wanted to reduce the amount of trash that was created. So instead of passing out plastic water bottles to runners, they gave them seaweed pouches filled with water. Once empty, the seaweed pouches could be eaten or thrown away to be biodegraded in just a few weeks.

AT SCHOOL

Start with these small changes, and your classmates might be inspired to join in. Set yourself a fun challenge to see how many friends you can get on board!

45 USE A PENCIL

A traditional wooden pencil is better for the environment than a pen. It's true that some mechanical pencils and pens can be reused and refilled over and over again. But at the end of the day, they're still made from plastic. And that plastic will sit on the planet or float in our ocean for decades while a pencil will turn into shavings that can be composted.

In the U.S. alone, 14 billion pencils and 6 billion pens are used each year!

If your school prefers pens, ask for a change! Explain why pencils are better for the environment.

46 CARE FOR YOUR STUFF SO YOU CAN REUSE IT

It's fun to buy new school supplies every year—but do you really need them? To help avoid creating unnecessary garbage, do your best to care for the supplies you already have and to not lose them. At the end of the school year, tuck your school supplies away nicely in your backpack so they are ready to go for your first day next year.

When you do shop for school supplies, pay attention to the packaging. Cardboard is always better than plastic, and no packaging is best of all! For example, an individual pencil with no packaging is better than a two-pack that's wrapped in plastic.

OUT AND ABOUT

When you're on the go, don't forget that you're on plastic patrol!

47 DON'T LITTER, AND PICK UP THE LITTER YOU SEE!

Because you care about the planet, you're probably not going to throw a plastic water bottle carelessly on the sidewalk. But sometimes littering isn't quite so obvious. Sometimes a plastic wrapper blows away while we're eating—go grab it! Other times you might be surrounded by trashcans when all you need is a recycling bin—hang on until you find one!

How many times have you walked past a plastic chip bag or soda bottle on the ground and thought, "Ugh! Why do people litter?" The next time you see plastic litter on the sidewalk, take those feelings one step further: pick it up and drop it in a recycling bin!

48 ORGANIZE A BEACH CLEANUP

Eighty percent of the plastic found in the ocean is blown out from land. That means it's especially dangerous when litter is found near the shores of oceans, rivers, and lakes. After all, many lakes and rivers eventually connect to the ocean.

Invite your friends and family to spend 30 minutes picking up trash along the shore. (Really, any bit of time will help!) Make it a competition by breaking into two teams and seeing who can collect the most items. Don't forget to separate the garbage from the recycling!

Even two minutes of beach clean-up can help. Check out **www.beachclean.net** to learn more about how even a couple minutes can make a big difference.

When you're at the beach, always keep track of your stuff. You don't want to leave behind a plastic frisbee or plastic beach ball that could easily blow into the ocean.

THE BIG PICTURE

In 1992, a ship set sail from Hong Kong to the United States. On deck was a huge crate filled with 28,000 plastic bath toys: ducks, turtles, frogs, and beavers. As the ship journeyed across the Pacific Ocean, something unexpected happened —the crate fell overboard.

The plastic animals bobbed thousands of miles across the ocean. Months later, they appeared on the beaches of Alaska. Years later, the "Friendly Floaties" were still being found in places like Scotland, Hawaii, and Australia. Thousands of them are still swirling around the ocean today.

When plastic litter gets tossed on the beach, you're not just littering your beach. You're littering beaches all over the world!

49 BUY LESS, OR DON'T BUY ANYTHING AT ALL

Souvenirs, jewelry, beauty products, and other little toys are fun to buy with your allowance. But they're often made of plastic. Before you buy something, ask yourself:

Do I really need it?

Do I have something at home just like it?

Can I borrow it instead?

And most importantly: is it made out of plastic?

Your money might be better spent saved up for a fun experience instead. (Also, see pages 90-97 for fun ways to make your parties waste-free and page 91 for ideas on low-waste purchases called consumables!)

PLANET PIONEER

What if you could pass down the things you didn't need anymore to someone who did need them? And it was free? People around the world are gathering together online and making it easier to do this.

The Buy Nothing Project and the Freecycle Network hope to keep perfectly good products out of the trash and put them into the hands of people who could use them. People who live close to each other organize into groups online. They post items that they don't want anymore or make a request for an item that they're looking for. People connect and arrange a pick-up time. Nothing is for sale and nothing lands in the trash. Learn more at **www.buynothingproject.org** and **www.freecycle.org**.

If your family is headed on a road trip (or even a short trip across town!), pack some snacks and sandwiches into a cooler with reusable food storage bags, silverware, and napkins. And don't forget refillable water bottles! If you don't have to eat at a fast food restaurant or pick up packaged snacks along the way, you'll avoid creating a lot of trash like to-go cups with lids and straws, plastic wrapping around snack items, and plastic silverware.

PACK A ZERO WASTE TRAVEL KIT

Keep one of these in the car or in your backpack, and you'll always have Earth-friendly options on hand. If you get hungry or thirsty while on the go, these items will reduce the amount of trash you and your family create:

- A refillable water bottle

- Reusable silverware

- Fabric napkin

- Metal straw

- Glass or metal food container

- Cloth shopping bag

51 GO PLASTIC-FREE WITH YOUR PET'S POOP

Do you help take your dog for a walk? If you do, that probably means that you help pick up dog poop, too. If your pet poops four times a day, that's 28 plastic pet waste bags that your family is tossing away each week! And we know that plastic film is not good for the environment. Convince your family to find a more Earth-friendly option. Search for a plastic-free bag that is compostable or dissolvable in water. If your dog poops close to home, you or a family member can consider picking it up with toilet paper then flushing it in the toilet.

PLANET PIONEER

Did you know you can turn poop into power? A dog park in the United Kingdom has a poop-powered street lamp. The lamp has an opening where pet owners can deposit their dog's poop. Then they turn a lever which stirs the mixture and creates heat. The poop naturally releases a gas called methane, which is collected until it's needed to power the light each night.

AT A PARTY

Celebrate with a few simple changes that will produce a lot less trash. Fancy gift wrapping can be tons of fun, but is it really worth all of the unnecessary waste?

52 GO GLITTER-FREE

Glitter is so fun, but it has a dark side: it's just tiny bits of plastic. And that messy microplastic can easily end up in the ocean after it's been washed down a drain. To be kinder to the environment, don't choose glitter party decorations, avoid face glitter, and skip wrapping paper or greeting cards with glitter.

53 GO GREEN WITH YOUR GIFT WRAPPING

Recycled paper, cardboard boxes, fabric pouches, and plain paper gift bags are much greener alternatives to wrapping paper. Wrapping paper that's glittery, metallic, fuzzy, or shiny can't be recycled. Instead, wrap a gift with recycled brown paper and decorate it with markers. Or, use a plain paper gift bag with plain tissue paper (remove the string handles before throwing it into the recycling bin).

There's one easy way to avoid waste when it comes to gift giving: give a consumable! A consumable is something that you can use up (or eat!) fairly quickly, like homemade cookies, candles, or DIY bath products such as a sugar scrub or lip balm in a reusable container.

Be careful— many gift bags and ribbons are made from plastic and can't be recycled.

HANG PAPER OR FABRIC PARTY DECORATIONS

54

Many party decorations are designed to be cheap and disposable, so they're often made from plastic. But things like plastic tablecloths and pennants can easily be replaced by fabric or paper. They look just as great, if not better, and they can be reused again and again. Hang on to them for your next party or lend them to a friend! Here are some ideas you can buy online, find at a craft fair, or make yourself:

☑ Paper streamers

☑ Yarn pom pom garland

☑ Tissue paper poufs

☑ Felt bunting

☑ Cloth banners

☑ Fabric table cloth

☑ Paper pinwheels

55 GIVE BETTER FAVORS

The cheap toys that you find in party favor bags or use as prizes for games are almost always made of plastic—and so are the favor bags they come in! Those kinds of toys might only get played with for a day or two before they eventually end up sitting in a landfill for years and years. Don't fall into that trap! Avoid throw-away plastic favors at your party as well as plastic party bags. Here are some things you can give instead:

Put these favors in a reusable fabric bag. Or skip the bag altogether! Flatpack cardboard gift boxes are also an option—and they can easily be decorated and personalized.

☑ Books (check out a used bookstore for deals)

☑ Craft supplies (that are used during the party for an activity)

☑ A small plant or seeds

☑ Journal and pencil

☑ Homemade cookies or treats

☑ Friendship bracelets

56 FORGO THE BALLOONS

A party without balloons? It's possible! Balloons are just another example of single-use plastic. Standard balloons are made from latex, which will biodegrade eventually in a landfill (but it could harm wildlife or marine life before it does). Shiny mylar balloons are made from a plastic that can be recycled, but is accepted by very few recycling programs. It won't biodegrade and could sit in a landfill forever.

Instead of decorating with balloons, here are some other ways to make your party feel festive:

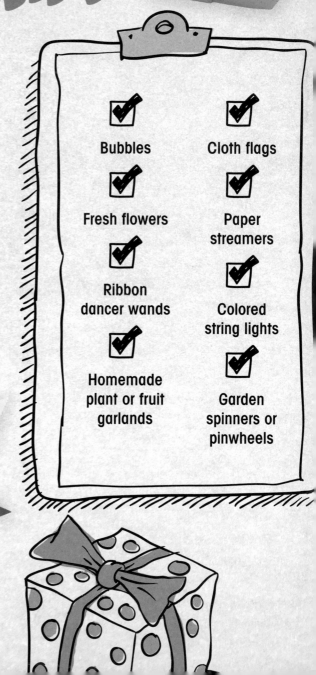

☑ Bubbles

☑ Cloth flags

☑ Fresh flowers

☑ Paper streamers

☑ Ribbon dancer wands

☑ Colored string lights

☑ Homemade plant or fruit garlands

☑ Garden spinners or pinwheels

Never do a "balloon release" where you let a bunch of helium balloons float away into the air. Those balloons will eventually deflate and end up in dirt, oceans, or trees where an animal, like a sea turtle, can eat it or get stuck in it. If you must use balloons, make sure each balloon ends up deflated in the trash where it belongs.

ECO CHALLENGE!

Make your next birthday party a zero waste birthday party! Use this chance to tell your friends all about why you want to create less waste and use less plastic. Maybe they'll want to try it themselves!

57 FORGET ABOUT DISPOSABLE DISHES

Plastic plates and cups are convenient but aren't great for the environment. It's best to use non-disposable plates and cups whenever you can. Besides not creating more garbage, there are a lot of benefits to using real dishes: they don't bend or soak through, you can't accidentally cut through them, and they're free—because they're already sitting in your cabinet!

But if you have to use disposable ones, look for dishware that's made from a material that's compostable like bamboo. When you're done, make sure they get thrown away in a compost pile. Paper plates might seem like a better choice, but any paper that's been stained with food can't be recycled. So, they'll end up in the landfill, too.

PLANET PIONEER

France was the first country in the world to ban disposable plastic dishes. Disposable plates, cups, and utensils can only be used if they are compostable and made from plant-based materials instead of petroleum-based materials. It's a big step in the right direction when it comes to the fight against plastic.

THE BIG PICTURE

Compostable and biodegradable items aren't always as great as they sound. Everything will biodegrade eventually—it just might take thousands of years! For example, in order for something to compost successfully, it needs to have soil, water, oxygen, and heat to break down. If it ends up in a landfill instead of a compost pile, it can't break down. That means a "compostable" plate could sit in a landfill for years! This is just another reason why reusable products are always better than disposable ones—even if they claim to be better for the environment.

AROUND YOUR COMMUNITY

The way you can make the biggest change is through your voice! Spread the word about the no-plastic movement and convince others to get involved.

58 SPEAK UP AT SCHOOL

School is the perfect place to spread the word about how to be more Earth-friendly.

Think of all those students. Together, you can make a huge impact!

Ask your teacher if you can give a presentation on how to reduce plastic waste, or if they can organize a school-wide assembly on the topic.

Bring this book to your school's library and see if they will order some copies, so other kids can learn how to reduce plastic.

Suggest a few plastic-free changes to your teacher or principal, like adding water fountains with bottle filling stations.

Make posters on recycling that clearly explain the rules and hang them up in your school cafeteria or canteen.

59

WRITE YOUR LOCAL REPRESENTATIVE

Your nearest city might already be considering laws that can help make your community more green. Or it may need some help thinking about the future. That's where you can come in! Visit your city's website to find out who you can send a letter or email to. Ask them to consider creating laws that will help reduce plastic like:

- Bans on plastic bags, straws, foam food containers, and plastic bottles.

- Taxes on plastic bottles and bags.

- "Straws only on request" rule for local restaurants.

- Expanded recycling program with more frequent pick-ups.

- City-wide composting service.

- Beverage container deposit laws (where customers get a refund when they return a plastic bottle).

- Safe, clean drinking water for all.

- Installation of more water fountains around the city.

60 SET AN EXAMPLE

Every time you make a choice to go plastic-free, your actions are making a statement. Take it a step further by explaining them. Your words combined with your actions may inspire others to re-consider their plastic polluting ways.

When someone offers you a plastic water bottle, you can say:

"No thanks. I'll refill my reusable water bottle instead. Every time I use it, that's one less water bottle that will end up in the ocean!"

When it comes to gifts, make the switch to asking for experiences instead of things. You could say:

"Instead of asking for a new toy for my birthday, I'm asking for a trip to the zoo. I'd rather make a fun memory with my family."

Your siblings, cousins, and friends may follow your lead.

ECO CHALLENGE!

Collect your family's plastic trash for one week in a recycling bin or separate bag. At the end of the week, count all the pieces. Then make it a goal to cut down on that number.

If you see someone throwing recycling into the garbage (or garbage into the recycling), you can say:

"Actually, that doesn't go there! Let me show you where it goes. It's better for the environment that way."

QUIZ!

Take this quiz to see if you're making the best choices...

#1 OR

A) REUSABLE WATER BOTTLE

B) PLASTIC WATER BOTTLE

#2 OR

A) SANDWICHES IN A BOX

B) SANDWICHES IN A BAG

#3 OR

A) LIQUID HAND SOAP

B) BAR OF SOAP

#4 OR

A) PLASTIC TOOTHBRUSH

B) BAMBOO TOOTHBRUSH

#5 OR

A) LARGE BAG OF CHIPS

B) LOTS OF SMALL BAGS OF CHIPS

#6 OR

A) REUSABLE TOTE BAG

B) SINGLE-USE PLASTIC BAG

#7 OR

A) HEAD OF BROCCOLI

B) PRE-CUT BROCCOLI FLORETS IN A BAG

#8 OR

A) PLASTIC SILVERWARE

B) METAL SILVERWARE

#9 OR

A) USING PLASTIC STRAWS IN DRINKS

B) DRINKING STRAIGHT FROM THE GLASS

TAKE THE "PLASTIC PATROLLER" PLEDGE!

Speak this aloud as a commitment to use less plastic and create less waste.

REFUSE!

I promise to say no to single-use plastic and spread the word!

RETHINK!

I promise to pick products with less packaging when I shop!

REPAIR!

I promise to care for and fix the things I already own before buying!

REUSE!

I promise to choose products that can be used more than once!

REDUCE!

I promise to buy less and think about whether I need new things or not!

RECYCLE!

I promise to put the planet first and recycle whenever possible!

Congratulations! You're officially a plastic patroller. The planet is counting on you to make a difference!

CHECKLIST

Here's a checklist of all the ideas in the book.
Tick them off when you complete each one.

IN YOUR BEDROOM

- [ ] **#1** Try to avoid plastic toys
- [ ] **#2** Buy used toys or borrow them
- [ ] **#3** Opt for experiences instead of toys
- [ ] **#4** Donate your toys
- [ ] **#5** Organize a toy swap
- [ ] **#6** Refuse fast food toys

IN YOUR CLOSET

- [ ] **#7** Take care of your clothing
- [ ] **#8** Get excited about hand-me-downs
- [ ] **#9** Wear cotton
- [ ] **#10** Choose secondhand
- [ ] **#11** Recycle your worn-out athletic shoes
- [ ] **#12** Don't chuck broken jewelry

IN THE BATHROOM

- [ ] **#13** Choose a better toothbrush
- [ ] **#14** Forget the toothpaste tube
- [ ] **#15** Sign up for a recycling program
- [ ] **#16** Buy bigger bottles
- [ ] **#17** Clean your ears with a cloth
- [ ] **#18** Add a recycling bin to your bathroom
- [ ] **#19** Switch to bars of soap
- [ ] **#20** Use solid body products
- [ ] **#21** Visit zero waste stores
- [ ] **#22** Make DIY bath bombs

AT LUNCH

- [ ] **#23** Replace your squeezable snack and juice pouches
- [ ] **#24** Switch to reusable zip bags and lunchbox containers
- [ ] **#25** Make homemade single portions
- [ ] **#26** Recycle properly
- [ ] **#27** Ditch plastic cutlery
- [ ] **#28** Give up gum!

OUT TO EAT

- [ ] **#29** Sip from the side!
- [ ] **#30** Pass on plastic to-go lids
- [ ] **#31** Order the cone instead of the cup
- [ ] **#32** Be proactive and say, "no, thank you!" to takeaway cutlery
- [ ] **#33** Forgo the to-go container
- [ ] **#34** Don't grab single-serve items
- [ ] **#35** Keep food out of the recycling bin
- [ ] **#36** Ask for a change

AT THE GROCERY STORE

- [ ] **#37** Bring your own reusable bag
- [ ] **#38** Skip the produce bags
- [ ] **#39** Buy in bulk
- [ ] **#40** Recycle plastic bags properly
- [ ] **#41** Pay attention to packaging
- [ ] **#42** Put pressure on wasteful companies
- [ ] **#43** Think twice about bottled water
- [ ] **#44** Filter your water without plastic

AT SCHOOL

- [ ] **#45** Use a pencil
- [ ] **#46** Care for your stuff so you can reuse it

OUT AND ABOUT

- [ ] **#47** Don't litter, and pick up the litter you see!
- [ ] **#48** Organize a beach cleanup
- [ ] **#49** Buy less, or don't buy anything at all
- [ ] **#50** Bring a cooler!
- [ ] **#51** Go plastic-free with your pet's poop

AT A PARTY

- [ ] **#52** Go glitter-free
- [ ] **#53** Go green with your gift wrapping
- [ ] **#54** Hang paper or fabric party decorations
- [ ] **#55** Give better favors
- [ ] **#56** Forgo the balloons
- [ ] **#57** Forget about disposable dishes

AROUND YOUR COMMUNITY

- [ ] **#58** Speak up at school
- [ ] **#59** Write your local representative
- [ ] **#60** Set an example

GLOSSARY

BAKELITE
The first fully synthetic plastic.

BIODEGRADABLE
Any material that can be broken down or can decay naturally into materials that are safe for the environment.

BPA
The abbreviation for bisphenol A. This chemical is often used in items such as water bottles, but BPA can seep into food and drink.

CELLULOID
A plant-based plastic invented in the 1860s.

COMPOST
Natural materials (like egg shells, coffee grounds, fruit peels, and leaves) that can be added to the soil where they will break down quickly and leave nutrient-rich soil.

COMPOSTABLE
Can break down into natural elements.

DECOMPOSITION
The process of something breaking down from its former state, or rotting.

DOWNCYCLING
Taking an item apart and reusing the different elements.

FOSSIL FUEL
A fuel, like oil or gas, that was formed in the Earth millions of years ago.

GREENHOUSE GASES
The gases released by burning fossil fuels. The release of these gases into the atmosphere contributes to climate change.

LANDFILL
A dedicated space where trash is buried then covered up with soil.

MICROPLASTICS
The name given to microscopic pieces of plastic that are now found in the oceans.

OCEAN DUMPING ACT
A law from 1972 that regulates the dumping of waste in the oceans.

POLYESTER
A common synthetic fabric that contains plastic.

POLYETHYLENE
Another name for polythene, this is the most common plastic in the world.

POLYPROPYLENE
A widely used plastic that can be reformed into pellets that can then be used to make new plastic items.

POLYSTYRENE
A light plastic often used in packaging.

POLYVINYL CHLORIDE
Commonly known as PVC, when this plastic is used to make containers it is recyclable.

RECYCLING
Converting waste material into reusable material.

RENEWABLE ENERGY
The name given to energy sources such as solar or wind that don't run out.

REUSE
A product gets used again for the same purpose it was originally intended for.

SYNTHETIC
An entirely man-made material.

UPCYCLING
Creatively improving and reusing items that might otherwise be thrown away.

ZERO WASTE
The aim of sending nothing to landfill by reducing, reusing, and recycling what you buy.

FURTHER READING

KIDS AGAINST PLASTIC

www.kidsagainstplastic.co.uk

This charity was set up by 16-year-old Amy and 14-year-old Ella. The website is packed with ideas and challenges for reducing plastic consumption so you can become "plastic clever".

HOW TO REDUCE PLASTIC AS A FAMILY

www.nationalgeographic.co.uk/environment-and-conservation/2018/06/reducing-plastic-family-easy-heres-how

Ten tips to share with your parents to help reduce your family's plastic use.

REDUCE, REUSE, AND RECYCLE TIPS FOR KIDS

www.reusethisbag.com/articles/reduce-reuse-and-recycle-tips-for-kids

A simple rundown of tips giving you practical ideas on how to reduce your impact on the Earth today.

PLASTIC SUCKS! YOU CAN MAKE A DIFFERENCE

by Dougie Poynter
(Macmillan Children's Books, 2019)

An accessible and friendly book on the threats that plastic poses to the planet and how you can make a difference.

101 SMALL WAYS TO CHANGE THE WORLD

by Aubre Andrus (Lonely Planet Kids, 2018)

A practical, fun, and creative book to inspire you to make a difference in the world. As well as tips for caring about the world, there are ideas to help you care for others and yourself.

ONE PLASTIC BAG: ISATOU CEESAY AND THE RECYCLING WOMEN OF THE GAMBIA

by Miranda Paul (Scholastic, 2017)

The true story of how one Gambian woman wanted to stop the plastic pollution that was ruining her community.

WHAT A WASTE: TRASH, RECYCLING, AND PROTECTING OUR PLANET

by Jess French (DK, 2019)

Everything you need to know about what we're doing to our environment. You will learn about how our actions affect the planet and what is being done to make things better.